And the Scroll Opened...

by George M. Lamsa

Drawings by Pat Ronson Stewart

DeVorss & Co., *Publishers*
P.O. Box 550
Marina del Rey, California 90291

Library of Congress Catalog Card Number 67-23820
Copyright © 1967 by George M. Lamsa
All Rights Reserved

First Paperback Edition, 1978
ISBN: 0-87516-274-6

Printed in the United States of America
by Book Graphics, Inc., Marina del Rey, California

To
Bill and Rebekah Upham
of St. Petersburg Beach, Florida.
As a token of my deepest and sincerest appreciation
for their kind interest in my work.

Contents

A Word about Ancient Worship	ix
1. The Shrine of Korra-Jenney	1
2. The Vision at the Sacred Stone	9
3. The First Scroll: About Love	13
4. The Second Scroll: About Marriage	21
5. The Third Scroll: About Children	25
6. The Fourth Scroll: About Sorrow and Happiness	29
7. The Fifth Scroll: About Religion	33
8. The Sixth Scroll: About Prayer	37
9. The Seventh Scroll: About Flowers	41
10. The Eighth Scroll: About Wealth	43
11. The Ninth Scroll: About Good Government	47
12. The Tenth Scroll: About Death	51
13. The Eleventh Scroll: About Freedom	57
14. The Twelfth Scroll: About Time	61
15. Crossing the Line into the Unknown	65
16. The Hereafter	75

A Word about Ancient Worship

Hidden in the mountain fastness of Kurdistan are the remains of some of the ancient Biblical customs and ways of life that have existed since the days of Abraham. These remnants of this ancient culture have been preserved like a precious object embedded in a piece of amber.

The inhabitants of this region, a part of what was once the Garden of Eden, still worship, pray, and sacrifice as their ancestors did in days of yore. They slaughter sheep and goats as offerings for the fulfillment of vows as the patriarchs did in the olden days. They pray at high places where they feel God's Presence is nearer just as Moses and Elijah had on Mount Sinai and Mount Horeb.

These ancient Biblical customs are so deeply rooted that the faithful travel miles to shrines and oracles, such as the temple at Korra-Jenney, in search of answers to the hidden forces that disturb their souls, and to find comfort, consolation, peace, and security.

During these ancient and sacred rites, the ecstasy of the soul and the yearning desire of the heart meet, and intense emotion causes the mind to cross the boundaries of limitless time and space. During such solemn hours, the prayers of the pilgrims pervade the crystal mountain air. And in these intense moments of meditation and fervent prayer, the past and present unite, the heaven and earth join hands, and the sun, moon, and stars shout with joy, for man is in touch with his Creator.

In the stillness and solitude of the shrines on the high places, man puts on his spiritual wings and rises like an eagle ready to fly into infinite space. Distance vanishes like wax before the fire, aye, like smoke that rises in the air. The past and present merge into the ecstasy of today, and memories of bygone days are quickened and made vivid.

In such hours of dedication and silent prayer, when the sweet savor of the soul rises like incense in the temple of God, the supplicant can hear strange voices, and, like a well-trained artist, depict real though unfamiliar images in his mind. With his inner eyes he can see Hannah, the mother of Samuel, beating her breasts, praying fervently, crying vehemently, and pouring out her heart to God in quest of a child. The supplicant can also see the high priest Eli sneering at her, mistaking her for a drunken woman, not realizing that on such dramatic occasions many sincere worshipers lose their sense of flesh, submerge into the unknown, and become drunk, not with wine, but with deep emotion caused by the burning flame of the heart's desire in its mystical approach to God.

Such were the memories of the sincere and faithful pilgrims who visited the shrine of Korra-Jenney and the sacred oracle near the town of Mar Bishoo each year. And such were the intense emotions and desires in their hearts that drew them to the isolated shrines in the high places and the silence and the solitude of nature so that they might commune with God.

These pilgrims, after offering their vows, dancing, and making merry, prayed in the silence of night when nature is asleep and God's voice is heard; when, in the stillness of night, the deep sleep falls upon the worshipers, time flees to its eternal place beyond the stars, and distance melts into the unknown. That is when the inner eye sees a glimpse of the world of reality, and the inner ear hears the voice of angels, God's messengers sent to answer prayers. It is then that the songs of joy and sadness mingle in the great cup that is held in the hands of the Lord of Life.

Such was the deep ecstasy of spirit into which the souls of the worshipers at the miracle stone were immersed when the man of God opened the ancient sacred scrolls and read their contents.

And the Scroll Opened...

CHAPTER 1

The Shrine of Korra-Jenney

North of the ancient city of Nineveh on the opposite bank of the Tigris River from present-day Mosul, and south of Mount Ararat, in the region of the Garden of Eden, in the long chain of the mountain fastness of Kurdistan, not far from the Turkish-Iranian border, lies the ancient town of Mar Bishoo and its large and historic cathedral. The town and cathedral are situated in a verdant valley. The area is surrounded by a range of high mountains which divides Turkey from Iran.

Nature has graced this "land of many waters" with verdant pastures, fruit trees, flowers, and a great variety of wild vegetables which grow uncultivated and unmolested by the human hand. Among these are the world-famous giant walnut trees. Indeed the land is a Paradise for its simple, pastoral, religious folk, whose main occupation is sheep and goat raising, and who live an outdoor life.

In the spring and summer months the tribes wander in the valleys and mountains carrying their tents and other household goods on the back of oxen and donkeys searching for pastures. During the cold months of winter they live in the valley in ancient stone houses built by their ancestors centuries ago.

The historic town of Mar Bishoo is noted for its colossal and ancient cathedral containing seven chapels for worship built by King Khoshap in the fourth century after Christ. This ancient edifice is the largest chuch in this land, which in Biblical days, because of its abundant water, fruit trees of many varieties, vegetables, rich pastures, and good climate, was called the Garden of Eden, which means "a delightful place."

This is the story of the building of this beautiful cathedral, which was, until recently, a great literary center where manuscripts and scrolls were written, old books copied, and young men educated for the priesthood.

King Khoshap hired a famous architect and his masons

to build the church. It was stipulated in their contract that the king would pay the architect a pound a week. When the king paid the architect, the latter gave it to the king's daughter, with whom he had fallen in love. She was the only and beloved child of the ruler. The princess, in turn, gave the gold coin to her father without any explanation, and her father paid the architect with it again, not knowing it was the same piece of money he had given him originally. This practice continued until the edifice was completed.

When the cathedral was ready to be dedicated, the architect called on the king and asked for his wages. The king in surprise stated that he had paid him every week. But when the architect told him that he had given the money to the princess, the king realized that it was the same coin which had changed hands throughout the building project. When the king's daughter told him she was in love with the architect and was saving the money for a dowry, the king smilingly looked at the builder and graciously consented to their marriage.

The grave of the princess is still to be seen in one of the chapels. It is visited by the sick, the mentally disturbed, the sufferers who seek healing and answers to their prayers. The author saw a violently insane man healed instantly. Missionaries were among those witnessing this miracle, and others have witnessed hundreds of such healings throughout the years.

The beautiful stone structure is visited from time to time by people from neighboring towns and from far-off places, who come to pray, to worship, and to fulfill their vows.

Nearby, there are many cells in the rocks and caves that once were inhabited by the men who had dedicated their lives to God and who in summer months visited the sheep camps in mountains and valleys. Some of them also had abodes high in the mountains.

On the southern side of the cathedral, near a rivulet, lies the grave of Raban Gamla, a holy man who devoted his life to the study of the word of God, and to prayer and meditation. The grave of this man of God is noted for a miraculous occurrence. Every year a large avalanche comes down from the high mountain and covers the graveyard, but not a flake of snow touches the grave of Raban Gamla. As the sliding snow reaches his grave it parts, and after passing it, joins again, leaving an island free from snow. This phenomenon occurs annually and is known to the people of the region.

In 1904, Mr. Langdon, an Englishman, visited Mar Bishoo in the springtime accompanied by the author and a few other students from the school. A few days after our arrival, the avalanche came down and the large, deep valley was filled with snow and rocks. We went with Mr. Langdon to see the grave and stood high upon the snow piles. As we looked down through the opening, behold, there was the grave of Raban Gamla without a flake of snow upon it!

For many years the people did not know why this spot was not covered by the snow but they felt something holy was there. A few years later, while digging a grave, the people discovered a slab of stone on which was inscribed, "This is the grave of Raban Gamla."

The Shrine of Korra-Jenney

The simple, pastoral people of the area (some of them the descendants of the ten tribes that were settled in these inaccessible mountains by the Assyrian kings in the eighth century B.C.) live just as their ancestors lived centuries ago. They still wear the same kind of shoes and clothes as their ancestors did in the days when the Hebrew patriarchs wandered throughout Palestine. They believe in healing; they revere the men of God and visit their graves and the places where they worshiped and prayed. They also believe in dreams, visions, and revelations, just as the Hebrew people did. They visit holy shrines, sacred stones and trees, sacrifice sheep, goats, and lambs as of yore. Moreover, they keep many of the customs, rituals, ordinances, and the tribal system which the Israelites kept before the captivity in 722 B.C. They, like the Israelites, offer gifts of food, sheep, and lambs to the men of God, who pray for them, heal their diseases, and bless them.

On the top of one of the highest mountains in the western range, several hours' journey from the town of Mar Bishoo, is an ancient shrine built of stone. It has four walls, a door, but no roof, and is called Korra-Jenney. The building is similar to the shrines which in Biblical days were called "high places." Probably it is one of the oldest remaining relics of the pre-Christian era.

This roofless shrine is visited yearly, late in August when the tribes, in order to escape the heat in the valleys, migrate to the plateaus where snow has been melting and fresh grass is still growing. The place is so high that it seems as though one is on the roof of the world.

The visitors to the shrine of Korra-Jenney are mostly shepherds, young people, childless women, newly married couples, and those whose hearts are heavy-laden.

An annual feast held in Korra-Jenney is celebrated by the people who live in nearby sheep camps. A great many people from towns also join them for the festival. A number of sheep, goats, and lambs are slaughtered and cooked, and the people pray, dance, eat, and make merry in the same manner as their ancestors did in Biblical days. This is one of the few occasions when the young men see and dance with their sweethearts, so it is a particularly joyful event for them.

On the top of a nearby mountain on the way between the town of Mar Bishoo and the shrine of Korra-Jenney is a large solitary stone resting in a vertical position. When the pilgrims visit Korra-Jenney they always stop to consult the sacred oracle. They pray and make their wishes known while kneeling before it.

The sacred stone is said to have rolled from its resting place on a high ridge down into the deep valley, and to have come back again miraculously to the ridge. It is a large, somewhat round stone, with one side thereof smooth; and is the only one of its kind found on the mountain ridge. It resembles a river stone.

For centuries, year after year, men and women have knelt and prayed before this sacred oracle, offering their prayers and making wishes. Some of them ask God to grant their wish for a child; some make supplications for prosperity and protection; young men petition God for good wives, and young maids pray for good and handsome husbands. Mothers pray for their children and for their husbands who are away, that the Lord God may bring them home safely and soon.

After the solemn prayers and loud supplications, with tears streaming down the cheeks, each person takes seven small, round pebbles from around the sacred stone and tries to fasten them one after another to the smooth side of the miracle stone, which rests at a vertical angle. The people believe that those whose round stones stick to the surface will have their prayers received and their wishes granted. In the case of those whose stones fall off, their wishes are not granted. As a result of many men and women succeeding in fastening their stones to the surface and having their prayers answered, the pilgrims' faith in the power of the stone has been enhanced over the years.

CHAPTER 2

The Vision at the Sacred Stone

And it came to pass on a feast day that a group of men and women had come to celebrate the feast of Korra-Jenney, and on their way back stopped at a lower ridge to pray before the miracle stone. On their arrival late in the evening, they prayed, made their wishes, and as the day grew older and the evening was nigh they wearily lay down and rested around the stone. Some of those whose supplications had not been granted in the years past continued to pray fervently with tears falling upon the stone, imploring God that their prayers be answered and their wishes granted.

As the shadows lengthened and the August day was spent, the last golden rays which the sun had thrown like a mantle upon the white and pale summer clouds disappeared, the moon and brilliant stars began to appear in the clear blue sky. When the darkness had fallen, the worshipers, now weary and tired of the day's activities, fell asleep.

At midnight, when nature's silence had fallen on the mountain, the man of God, who centuries before had spent many lonely years of his life in the mountains fasting and praying, appeared in a vision behind the miracle stone with a bundle of ancient, sealed scrolls in his arms. And he said, "I know you all." Then he added, "Oh, how many moons have waxed and waned, and how many summers have been replaced by cold winters, and I have yearned to see your faces and to hear the echoes of the prayers of your departed parents uttered through your lips."

He placed the scrolls upon the stone and then he stretched forth both of his hands as though trying to embrace them, and he continued: "I know why you have come here; I have hearkened to your prayers and I know your heart's desires. Verily, I say to you, the same forces and emotions that made your parents ascend this high mountain, to worship and to make supplications before God,

The Vision at the Sacred Stone

have also brought you here. For you are the fruits of prayers and wishes of your parents whom I have often seen praying before this sacred stone. At that time you were the hidden secrets in their hearts and the unfulfilled desires of their souls. Now you have quickened the memory of your departed parents and brought back their granted wishes. And now your lips utter their prayers and your hearts are filled with their emotions.

"For on this historic and sacred stone the tears of joy and sorrow mingle, and the past and the future merge into the present. Verily, I say to you, the departed souls of your ancestors who prayed and made supplications for your birth, rejoice with you; and they see this sacred stone with your eyes; they hear my voice with your ears, and they play on the strings of your harp with your hands, and sing their melodies with your voices.

"In the past I have spoken to them, when you were the buds in their hearts, and now I will speak to you and impart some of the secrets of life which I have learned from these ancient scrolls in my cave of solitude and on this lonely and beautiful mountain."

CHAPTER 3

The First Scroll: About Love

And as he was through speaking, and nature had spread its gray mantle upon the valley and deep slumber had fallen upon the worshipers, a scroll was opened—and its contents were about love. And he read:

"Love is the hidden force which at birth binds your body and your soul together, until it separates them at death.

Yea, it is the key which opens the petals of your heart and lets the flowers unfold before the sun, so that the sweet fragrance may ascend as an offering to the God of Life."

Then he continued:

"Love is an eternal debt which one generation owes to another. Aye, even the kings and the princes are not exempt from it. It is a debt that is beyond the power of the rich to pay. For you give that which was given unto you by your parents and you measure that which was measured unto you to your children."

Then he raised his voice with emotion and strange tones and said:

"Oh love, where is your hiding place, and where does your magic touch dwell? The sea says, 'It is not in me, for my depths are measurable and my shores are limited.' The mountain says, 'My peaks are too low and humble for love to dwell upon them, and my foundations are too weak to hold its weight.'

"Verily, I say to you, love is a sun that never sets beyond the horizon and a dawn that is never darkened. The ways of love are hidden even from the wise and prudent, and its footsteps are obliterated by strong winds and storms. Aye, love is like a ship without a rudder and compass, like a wayfarer lost in a vast desert. And its ways are like a deep and shoreless sea.

"Oh, how sweet and sorrowful are the melodies of its music, and how the whole of nature responds to the mysterious sounds of its drums and dances to the hidden tones of its flute! And all men and women drink from the cup of mixed wine which love constantly holds in its hands; both the prince and the slave drink alike.

"In truth, I say to you, let love fly into the air with the fragrance of the summer rose and let the sorrowful tears mingle with tears of joy.

"The chains with which love binds your body and soul together are stronger than fetters of iron and steel. For love ascends to the stars and penetrates the depths of the grave. It is like the water which causes the clay to stick together even after the earthen vessels are burned in the furnace. Aye, the chains of love remain unbroken and its secrets undiscovered. Love lives even when bodies have turned into dust.

"Nevertheless, just as love molds you, shapes you, and nourishes your desires, and binds your heart and soul together, so it separates you one from another. The same cohesive force that draws you close to each other and causes you to embrace one another, also makes you forget your parents, and friends of your youth. Yea, it even compels you to forsake the tender breasts that once poured out their strength into your hungry veins, and the tender arms that held you firmly to the bosom. The same love that unites you before the altar separates you at the grave, and then flies into space chanting your songs and playing on the harp of your soul.

"Let love, therefore, unite your heart and soul together. Let love stir you up like the ripening wheat is stirred up by the gentle and soothing waves of the warm summer wind, but let not its force rend your hearts asunder. For great and infinite is the power of love, and its paths are unchartered. Its ways are subtle like the way of the wind, no one knows whence it comes and where it goes; and yet it always comes and always goes. Yea, love is like an endless road and a journey without destination. Even the wise and crafty are lost in it.

"Verily, I say to you, love is the wine of the soul. Let your cup be filled with it, but not to the brim, for love is too precious to be spilled on the ground and trodden under foot. True love is the pure fountain of life from which both the wise and the pure in heart have drunk and found eternal joy.

"Therefore, let love nest in your heart securely until its wings grow and it is ready to fly. Once love is on its wings, it may fly; and if your nest is not garnished it may never return to you again.

"And truly I say to you, you must transcend physical passion and build a new spiritual nest in your heart so that love may fly back and remain in your heart, until at last it separates your body from your soul and flies to its secret place.

"Again I say to you, your yearning desires, your embraces, and your deep emotions are caused by the inarticulate cries of the unborn generations, who are impatiently waiting for their round, to drink from the sweet and bitter cup of life and to dance in the great feast of the union of the earth and the stars and the sun. Even though their sinews are not formed, their voices are heard through your voice and their silent songs are played on the chords of your harp, for they dwell in your heart. Aye, they are your dreams of today, and your fulfilled desires of tomorrow.

"Now, hearken unto me! Love is the sweet and hidden pollen which is nesting in the tender and secret petals of your heart waiting to be awakened by the silent and sweet tones of your soul. Its fragrance invites you to a great feast wherein two blends of wine made from the vineyard that was planted by the hand of God are mixed together and are ready to be drunk. And the more is drunk, the more the joys of life abound.

"Love is like a prolific river that constantly pours out its waters but never exhausts its source. Its depths are like those of a fathomless sea. Aye, love is a deep well from which the thirsty and weary wayfarers drink and revive their soul. It is a hope for the hopeless and a joy to the mourners. In love you embrace the souls which have drunk their round and gone, and you kiss the lips of those who are waiting to drink from the cup and to respond to the sweet and sad melodies of nature.

"Oh, my brothers and sisters! Let the joys of your love nest deep in your heart, so that he who drinks from your well and lodges in your inn may find comfort and rest for his soul. For the journey of life is long and the true paths that lead to the eternal way of life are thorny.

"Yea, the secret of love is wisdom and the key to its chambers is imagination. Your mind cannot grasp what your eyes see, and your eyes cannot see the borders of your imagination. Love, like the light and the air, has neither limits nor boundaries. The sea is its footstool and the stars are its pavilions, but its paths are hidden. Yea, the bird knows the ways of the air; the fish knows the dark paths of the deep, but the ways of love are a mystery and its secrets are locked in eternity—for love was never created, neither does it die.

"And again I say to you, only in love do the finite and the animate become infinite and immortal. Love carries you on its wings and causes you to cross the shoreless seas. Aye, at times love makes you to drink from its sweet and bitter cup. It carries you to verdant pastures where earthly pleasures abound, and at times, in order to test your strength, it drops you as strong wine does and leaves you on the ground.

"Every seer and sage will tell you that love is like a two-edged sword—it cuts both ways. Out of the bitter comes the sweet. Your joys of today may be the seeds of your sorrow of tomorrow. For as the day is followed by the night, and the light by darkness, joy is followed by sorrow.

"There is an end to every ladder that you may climb, and a destination for every journey. But love has no limits nor end, nor can its depths and heights be reached or measured. Yea, love is like an underground river: no one knows its source or its destination, and only those who go deep, and the wise, can drink of its pure and inexhaustible waters.

"The music of love is sweet and its silent voice soothing. All of those who have responded to the strange sound of its drums and danced to the rhythms of its flute have been drowned in its depths.

"Truly, I say unto you, love flies with the wings of the

light. It climbs the tree of life until it reaches the tender boughs. Its depth is deeper than the ocean; its imprints are in the sea and its paths in the air. Only time can tell its course; only faith can reveal its destination. Love is like a seed. It sleeps secure in the winter, dreaming of warm spring when the gentle sun rays quicken it and adorn it with glory and the visiting bee seeks its life-giving nectar.

"In the words of the great poet and philosopher, King Solomon: 'For love is as strong as death; desire is as cruel as Sheol; its flashes are flashes of fire and flame.'"

CHAPTER 4

The Second Scroll: About Marriage

And when the darkness had fallen upon the earth and the deep silence had replaced the solitary crying of shepherds and the chattering of birds, another scroll opened, and its contents were on marriage. And the man of God opened his mouth and read:

"In marriage your wandering souls unite once more, to

dwell together in the strange and temporal inn of life. The soil from which the sinews of your bodies were formed joins together again, so that another offering from the fragrance of your garden may be offered to the God of Light.

"Verily, I say unto you, in your marriage you become a burning candle from which myriads of candles will be lighted to illuminate the Great Temple of God.

"In truth, your bodies are made of clay, but your souls came from beyond the stars. And in this union the mortal and the immortal unite and the infinite temporarily become finite, and the inanimate articulates and shouts with joy. Even the gods share in your feasting, and the earth and the planets join in your union. And the stars dance at your wedding feast, for they join hands through you and kiss one another with your lips, and at your death they separate once more to be joined again.

"In your union let your lamps be burning like the sun and keep your vessel full of the precious oil, for your journey is long and its destination uncertain. Myriads of the unborn are holding their candles and are waiting for their time to light them from your candles and to fill their vessels from your precious oil so that they may participate in the great feast—the drama of life—and drink from the same cup from which you have drunk.

"And I say unto you, Beware that your earthen vessels may not break and the precious oil made by the hands of God spill and your lights be put out.

"And, in marriage, let your wine mix and your sweet fragrance blend and your voices sing in harmony. And when the day is warm, let the petals of your souls open so that the precious perfume of your flowers may fill the air. For when autumn comes your flower will dry up, but your sweet fragrance will still be in the air, and the sound of the trumpets of your hearts will gladden the hearts of those who are waiting for their round to drink from the Wine of God, and to walk on the paths which your feet have trod.

"Mother earth rejoices to hear your voices and to feel the touch of your feet, and its inanimate soil is glad to become the flute through which the voice of the Creator is heard and the cup in which His own hands had mixed the sweet wine, and the invisible spirit took form and became visible.

"In truth, long before you were united before the altar, your bodies were fashioned. Yea, before the waves of the sea reached the distant shores and kissed the soil, and your inner candles were lighted; before the planets started to revolve in their orbits; before the first ray of the sun struck the earth."

CHAPTER 5

The Third Scroll: About Children

And as the night grew older and the thick darkness covered the earth, and new and familiar stars appeared in the brilliant skies, another scroll was opened and its contents were about children. And he continued to read:

"Your children are your fulfilled dreams and your hearts'

tender buds nourished with your love. The warmth of April, the month of blossoms, has caused them to bloom.

"Now let your tender and green petals open slowly, so that the warmth of the April sun may nourish the flower. And when your flowers are in full bloom, the summer will water them with its precious dew and fill them with fragrance and cause their fruit to ripen.

"Verily, I say to you, your children are the offerings which you offer to the Creator, and the little candles you hold in your hands to be placed in the Great Temple of the Spirit.

"Like a tree that silently and securely holds its fruit at the top of its tender branches to be nourished by the sun, so you hold them high in your arms and nourish them with your love. For once you yourself were gently borne in the tender arms of your parents and nourished with their sweet love. Verily, I say unto you, you only render to your children that which your parents have rendered to you, and you guard the precious light which they have entrusted unto you.

"The same mystic power that nourishes the trunk of a tree also nourishes the branches and designs the flowers and causes the fruit thereof to ripen. Your love for your children is the same love wherewith your parents have loved you, and your light is their light and the flame of their candles is still burning in your candles, and their hearts' desires rest in your heart.

"In truth, your children are your tender and abundant spring blossoms wherein the precious fruit of life is nestling.

And when the wind causes some of them to drop off, do not grieve over them. And when you weep do not say, the gods of nature have been cruel and unjust because they caused some of your flowers to wither and a few of your fruits to drop off. For the gods have their share in your sacrifices and sweet offerings and a share of the fruit of your vineyard. Aye, the generous and good husbandmen leave some of the grapes on the vine for the hungry and weary wayfarer and for birds and insects. And the generous reapers let some of the precious wheatears drop on the ground for the needy gleaners. For the wayfarer and the birds also have a share in the labor of your hands and a portion of your bread.

"And again, I say unto you, the children whom you lose are the cut flowers from your spring garden to grace the altar in the Great Temple of Life. Aye, their passing is like eventide, which suddenly disappears. Your hearts are sorrowed by their sudden departure, but the Tree of Life that entrusted them to you rejoices at their return and is happy to feel their fresh petals and smell the fragrance of the young open rose.

"Just as you admire the fresh flowers of your garden which your own hands have planted and cultivated, so the gods love the labor of their own hands. And the same hand which carefully planted the rose and watered it, also cuts it off. And when it is cut off the mother plant is temporarily shorn of its glory, but the fragrance of its flowers fills the air and its beauty graces the altar of God.

"Consider the trees in your gardens, how securely they

hold the fruit they bear; yet some of it drops off before its season, so that the other may mature and ripen. Verily, I say unto you, the tree is aware of every fruit that drops off, and its silent ears hear the sound of every leaf when it strikes the ground, and it understands the mysteries of nature, and is aware that nothing perishes and that nature knows no losses. For a single apple on a tree, good, and well ripened, is sufficient to fill the earth with myriad trees of its kind.

"Not all men are blessed with children, but all humanity rejoices in them. Children are like beautiful flowers in a field coveted by the eyes of both the owner and the stranger. For not every branch of a tree blossoms, but the whole tree is decorated with the flowers, and all branches share in making them.

"Yes, it is not the number of children that you bring into the world that counts, but it is the quality of your fruit that pleases the eye of the Owner of the Orchard.

"Therefore, when one of your dear ones leaves this life, do not mourn, but say, 'I will make of you a bouquet of flowers to be placed permanently before the throne of the God of Life.'"

CHAPTER 6

The Fourth Scroll: About Sorrow and Happiness

And as the night silence reigned and man's inner ear opened, another scroll opened, and its contents were about happiness. And after a brief silence the man of God opened his mouth and read:

"In the cold winter months nests the desire of the warm,

soothing months of the distant spring. For out of a raging storm comes calm, and out of war, peace.

"As the sun starts to return from its journey southward, the cold winds of the north flee before the warm and soothing winds of the south. And then nature once more adorns the earth with glory and majesty; the long winter silence is broken with shouts of joy.

"Verily, I say unto you, your joys and happiness are conceived in the inner chambers of your suffering and sorrows, and your shouts of joy are the sweet and the sad melodies which were hidden in the depths of your heart and nursed with your inner desires. Your laughter of today pours out of your sorrows of yesterday, just as the shining color comes out of a burnished piece of brass after it is heated in the furnace. Your joys and happiness are borne on the wings of your sorrow.

"Yea, happiness and sorrow are inseparable—one preceding the other like the day and night—like the seed and the tree. Aye, they nest securely together and they embrace one another, and when they are spiritually understood they become twin sisters or the two ends of a measuring line. Joy and sorrow are like different colors in a flower, which are nourished by the same stem and roots and breathe the same air.

"For the same victory which brings joy to the heart of the conqueror brings sadness to the heart of the defeated.

"In truth, I say unto you, the deeper the sorrow plants its seed in your heart, the stronger and more lasting is your future joy. Aye, the joys of the sower are conceived and

The Fourth Scroll: About Sorrow and Happiness

born during the cold winter months, when precious seed which he had scattered on the ground rises in the springtime with glory and majesty. For it is the grim darkness of the night that gives birth to the magic of the dawning of the day, and it is the pain and travail, even the sound of the footsteps of death, that herald the joy of the birth of a child.

"Your happiness is the dream of your sleeping sorrows, and your sorrows are the shadows of your absent joys. And when you are sad you play on the finer chords of your instruments, and both your happiness and sorrows bring tears to your eyes, for the secret chamber of both lie in your heart, just as in the black chambers of coal are hidden the light and the colors of the sun.

"The sorrows of the hungry sower in the spring, who weeps as he scatters the precious seed in the ground while his children are hungry, are the joys of the hungry reaper who feasts during the harvest season.

"Happiness is the verdant frontier of your imagination. Yea, it is the unblossomed flowers in the hidden garden of your heart. Happiness is like a wilderness without a horizon and a sea without shores.

"In happiness and sorrow hold your standard high and let not your desire die, and let not the rose which your heart had nourished dry. Neither let the flame of your candle vanish into the endless sky."

CHAPTER 7

The Fifth Scroll: About Religion

Now the night was growing old, the moon was setting, and the brilliant morning stars began to throw their mantle upon the sky. The stillness was broken by the barking of dogs and the chattering of birds. Another scroll opened, and its contents were about religion. And the man of God opened his mouth and read:

"Verily, I say unto you, your religious emotions are caused by your lost freedom, and through your worship and prayers you fly by unseen wings of the spirit to the former places wherein you dwelt before your immortal souls inhabited your mortal bodies—before the inanimate and the animate joined hands. Aye, before they started to sing in the great symphony of life.

"Once you flew with the wings of spirit and you lived above the earth in peace and tranquillity and watched the storms and tempests below you, and now in your religious emotions you try to retrace your footsteps and find your lost wings, and fly again.

"In truth, I say unto you, your thoughts of prayer and worship are born through your visions of a lost Paradise; they are the dreams of a happy yesterday, which now are awakened by your true desires and stirred by the strong winds and fears of the unborn tomorrow. Aye, I can liken you to a bird that has lost its wings, that is dreaming of the days it crossed the seas and looked down on the peaks of mountains.

"Your true concept of religion is the spiritual pattern of your heavenly habitation and of the uncorruptible garment in which you were clothed before your feet trod the dust of this earth, before good and evil were known and the words for glory and shame were coined.

"In your meditation, for a while, you take off your earthly garments and stand naked and shameless before the God who fashioned your bodies, and then you put on the wings of the spirit wherewith you fly to the outermost ends of the universe. For in prayer, you become one with the universe and in the stillness of night you converse with angels, aye, with God.

"And I say unto you, the temple which your hands have built is not the true place where God dwells, but a place wherein you meet Him and converse with Him. Because only when you dress in your natural and spiritual garments and remove your shame can you come into the presence of the King. And when you pray in silence you see your real self. Verily, I say to you, God can only see you as you were created, dressed in white robes, pure and perfect.

"Your places of worship are the secret chambers wherein temporarily you strip yourself of your earthly garments and stand naked in your real self. For God loves to see your soul and feel the touch of the work of His hands, like a potter rejoices when he feels the touch of his vessel.

"Aye, once you were free from the fears and cares of this turbulent and mortal life. Heaven was your habitation, nature was your constant companion, and the sun, moon, and stars rejoiced to see your beautiful bodies, and the still and silent trees of the forest envied you when you walked. Sickness and sorrow fled from your presence and mother earth embraced you in her tender arms. Yea, at that time you feared no one and you worshiped no one. Then you were free like the air and the sun. You were princes—children of the Most High.

"And I say to you, let your inner temple be your heart and your outer temple the sky; and let the trees and flowers of the field be your companions, and let the sun and the moon be your candles so that your heart can be lighted with wisdom and understanding. When your inner temple is lighted, the outer veil is removed; then you become one with spiritual forces.

"Your priests are the dreams of yourselves when you were clothed in your real white garments unblemished, ready to attend the great feast and to see the face of the King. Yea, they helped you to see your real self. For once you were purer than the crystal and whiter than the snow. Your priests can help you but they cannot carry your burdens through the narrow paths of this life. They can teach you to fly, but they cannot give you wings to rise into the air.

"Would that I could destroy the fear which nests in your heart and cut the chains which bind you to this earth. Would that I could teach you the hidden ways of the air and the secret paths of the deep, so that you might be able to ride upon the turbulent waves and look from above and laugh at the stormy sea below. Would that I were able to give you the wings wherewith to fly to the green pastures and heavenly places where fears and desires vanish and peace and harmony reign."

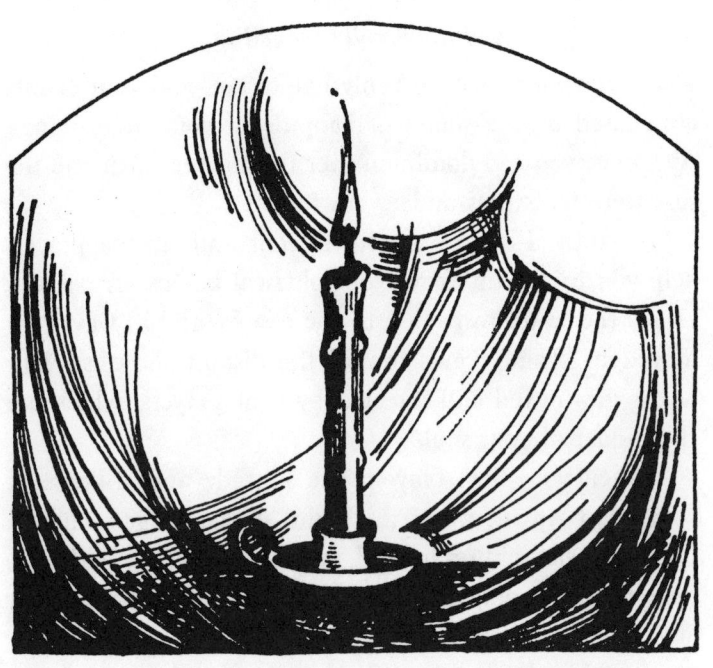

CHAPTER 8

The Sixth Scroll: About Prayer

And when the first curtain was lowered and another curtain lifted up, and darkness was giving way to the dawn, and early dewdrops were falling upon the dry summer grass, another scroll opened, and its contents were about prayer. And again the man of God opened his mouth and read:

"Your prayers are the dreams of your imprisoned souls

which crave for their heavenly habitation, and your chants are caused by the sound of flapping of your inner wings. Aye, once you had dominion over the air; the earth and the seas were footstools under your feet.

"In truth, I say unto you, fervent and sincere prayers help you to rise up above your physical bodies just as heat causes the water to rise up to the clouds, and as waves are moved by strong winds toward the distant shore, so your hearts are moved and directed by your prayers, which are the rudder of your soul.

"When you pray, pray in the solitude and stillness of your heart—in silence of the night, in the tongue wherein the angels sing praises to God, and God converses with you. And when you pray do not ask, for in asking you show your lack and ingratitude to the Lord of Life, who meets all your needs and heals your wounds. You cannot ask for what you already have. Yea, the king's favors are not solicited but bestowed upon his worthy subjects. Aye, what nourishes the roots nourishes the branches and the leaves, and what is in heaven is already on earth within your reach.

"In your prayers become like a sweet fragrance so that you may ascend before the throne of God and present your body as a holy temple worthy to be visited by the King. For your prayers cannot serve to counsel God and change His attitude toward you, but it changes your own heart and lets the harmony of your songs touch the hearts of those for whom you pray. For you cannot paint a flower with better and more harmonious colors than those with which the gentle hand of the God of Life has adorned it. Nor

The Sixth Scroll: About Prayer

can your prayers cause the rays of the sun to be warmer or the ocean to supply the clouds with more vapor. The ocean gives what the rivers bring in and the rain pours out that which the clouds had received. Your needs were met before your feet trod the earth and your prayers answered before you knelt in the temple.

"For the same power which had supplied your needs yesterday is able to meet them tomorrow. Pray before the darkness falls and misfortune strikes its sharp teeth; before poverty replaces prosperity and sickness takes the place of health.

"For in prayer your inner eye sees the unseen and your inner ears hear that which lies in the deep silence. Aye, your prayers ride on the wing of the spirit and embraces the boundless universe.

"Pray that you may be taught how to share that which God has already entrusted to you, so that you may know how to receive. For the same key that unlocks the heart of the giver opens the heart of the receiver. And when you bless others, your blessings are multiplied unto you, just as the seed that the sower scatters on the ground is multiplied a hundredfold.

"Verily, I say unto you, your Father in heaven loves to see you assembled together and to hear your silent voices. And the wind loves to carry your harmonious melodies beyond the seas. The God of Life rejoices to watch you light your candles in this earthly temple and to see you drink from the abundant Cup of Life. Just as a tree is proud of its leaves and flowers, so God is delighted in you.

"When you pray, let your heart open like the spring flowers, ready to receive the warmth of the sun, and let your prayers ride on the wings of spirit. God is not deaf and nature speaks, hears, and feels the gentle drop of the spring rain. Pray quietly when nature is resting from its toil and when God is speaking. For prayer is the compass of your rudderless ship and the pilot of your weary soul. For in prayer new songs break forth from the unknown and you search for the unsearchable and you try to fathom the unfathomable. And when your prayers are answered, new prayers spring forth from the well of the Living Water."

CHAPTER 9

The Seventh Scroll: About Flowers

And when the silence of the early dawn was broken by the calling of partridges, and the fires of shepherds began to be seen on the mountainside, another scroll opened, and its contents were about flowers. And the holy man opened his mouth and read:

"Flowers are the earth's desires conceived during the cold

winter months and born in the springtime to adorn mother earth with glory and majesty.

"Verily, I say unto you, the colorful array of fragrant flowers is the earth's thank offering to God for the returning of the sun rays which have adorned it with beauty and glory.

"Just as you express yourselves with beauty, music, and prayers, so the earth arrays itself with flowers and speaks with colors. Yea, it greets the sun god with a warm smile and fills the air with sweet perfume so that all creatures may share its joy. For every flower that the earth brings forth to sing praises, the sun sends myriads of warm rays.

"Oh, how beautiful and comely are the flowers in desert places and how sweet is the sound of waterfalls in a dry land. Flowers grace the altars and shrines and decorate the tables of princes and nobles. They silently come and silently go. They give everything but take nothing and they make no claims.

"Flowers are the incarnated sun; their beautiful colors are the light of God manifested in nature. Therefore, the flowers' only desire is to grace the altar of God who has clothed them with beauty and majesty, and to share their fragrance with all of God's creatures.

"Oh, how sweet is the sound of your music and how soothing is the touch of your feet, O bee! For when you gently alight on the colorful carpet which the flowers have spread for the silent touch of your feet, you quicken life in it and scatter its seed over the earth."

CHAPTER 10

The Eighth Scroll: About Wealth

Now when the eastern sky became bright like silver, heralding the break of day, another scroll opened, and its contents were about wealth. And the man of God opened his mouth and read:

"Wealth is the gift of the God of Life entrusted to those who know how to guard it and how to distribute it to His children. As a tree is mindful of all the branches and leaves thereof, so the God of Life is mindful of all His creations.

"In truth, I say unto you, wealth is like the air, light, and water. You can use it and keep it for a while, but you have no control over it. For wealth is like changing winds and shifting sands; lo, today it is here, tomorrow there. Its course is mysterious, it changes hands. Today it is your guest and tomorrow it belongs to another one. Aye, not even kings have control over it.

"Wealth is like a prolific river—it must flow. It is like an ocean ready for all who are courageous to sail upon its turbulent waves. Only the wise navigators and the brave merchants have been able to possess it and keep it temporarily. Wealth flees like a bird that escapes the snare of the fowler.

"The source of wealth is in the sun, air, and the rain. Yea, wealth is like a stream flowing on dry land. It must have channels in order to irrigate the soil. Wealth is like a crown which is studded and adorned with precious jewels; it graces the head of the king, but also it brings honor and glory to the whole state. The crown belongs to the state, and the power of the ruler is derived from the people. Yea, many are contestants for the crown, but only a few are privileged to wear it. Many are the seekers of the wealth, but only few can find it and hold it for a time.

"In truth, wealth is like a desert well belonging to the prince of the tribe, but its water is drunk by all members of the tribe, and shared with strangers and weary travelers. For mother nature is mindful of all and provides for all.

"Therefore, let your wealth flow like swift currents of a river in the springtime and let your love for humanity fill the air like the sweet fragrance of a Persian garden of roses in summertime. For the river that pours out its water abundantly flows even in the dry months of summer.

"There is a limit to the seas, but there is no limit to human aspirations, and no boundaries to human greed and desire for more wealth. Yea, what mind can conceive, the eye cannot see; and what the eye can see, the hand cannot grasp. To try to possess wealth and to stop its flow is like one trying to harness the wind and reduce the speed of light and control the heat of the sun.

"Wealth is the concrete rays of the sun that the god of nature has stored in substances ready to provide sustenance for God's creations; and the same winds that collect it in one place, scatter it to the far-off corners of the earth."

CHAPTER 11

The Ninth Scroll: About Good Government

The dawn had broken but the weary pilgrims were still asleep around the sacred stone as men who had been overcome with strong drink. And another scroll opened, and its contents were about good government. And the man of God opened his mouth and read:

"Your government is a weak temporary shelter which you

yourself have created in the anticipation of heavy rains and storms. Yea, it is like a shepherd's tent; today it is struck here and tomorrow it is struck in another place. Your government, good or bad, is the result of your own deeds and actions and no one is responsible for it but you yourselves. The fetters which bind your hands and feet have been fashioned by your own hands. For it is the lust of the bird that causes him to be caught in the snare of the fowler.

"I have often likened you to little children playing with clay, building vessels and breaking them. For like children, you lack the magic touch of the fingers of the potter who glories in the workmanship of his hands. And, I say unto you, your temporal laws and ordinances are a mental fence that you erect around you. Yea, they are like a spider's web, which cannot withstand strong winds, nor offer protection to its weaver.

"Your dreams of good government, freedom, and self-determination are aroused by your thoughts of the loss of your real world. For once you were free from all the burdens of this temporal life, and stood erect like the strong and tall cedars of Lebanon, and mountains and hills were proud to look at your height. The good earth nourished your roots, the mountain streams watered you, and the strong winds and severe storms could not break you.

"But now your own weight has bent your boughs to the ground and broken some of your tender branches. Your government is your own shadow and the fruits of your actions. No one can rest under his own shadow. Your laws are a covering to hide your transgressions against nature's laws.

"Verily, I say unto you, you are all princes, the sons of the Most High God and the precious flowers which the earth has produced. You were not born to be misruled and oppressed one by another; or the weak to be devoured by the strong; nor the simple deceived by the cunning. For the judge who condemns you today may be found in the same predicament tomorrow.

"Consider the trees of the forest and the lilies of the field, how they stand erect like princes and kings on their ground; breathing the air and receiving nourishment from the sun freely."

CHAPTER 12

The Tenth Scroll: About Death

And toward the early morning, when the eastern horizon was red like crimson and the birds were chirping their greeting to the first rays of the sun, another scroll was opened, and its contents were about death, and the man of God opened his mouth and read:

"Death is a temporary separation of the body and the

soul; the articulate and the inarticulate. Yea, it is the dismantling of a shepherd's tent in the autumn month when the summer is over, when the sheep camps move homeward and the birds migrate southward.

"Death is caused by breaking the strong chains fashioned by the fingers of God that bind you in the womb; it is the same mysterious key that at your birth locked the intricate padlock wherewith the magic touch of nature's fingers joined your body and soul together.

"Verily, I say unto you, death is the departure of the divine intelligence that in the outset had caused the inanimate matter to think and speak, and the formless dust to take form and walk. Yea, I liken death to the precious drops of rain that fall on the ground, flow into the meandering streams which finally carry them in turbulent currents until they rest in the Great Sea of Life. When you die, you reach your destination, and the great and calm Ocean of Life, which permitted your departure, is glad to embrace you and receive you back again.

"Your death was decreed from the very day you were conceived; when you entered the great but temporary inn. As a sojourner is mindful of his departure, so you were mindful of your coming journey. Every tree that is planted is cut off, and every flower that is ready to bloom in the spring is mindful of the frost of the autumn, and the same warm sun's rays which nourish the rose and array it with beauty, also cause it to wither and fade away.

"In truth, there are four seasons in the year, and for every cold day in the winter there is a warm summer day; and

The Tenth Scroll: About Death

yet there are the soft winds of the spring and the pleasant days of autumn.

"Only those who are not born will not die, and only the seeds that are not sown will escape the reaper's sickle. Aye, death is not a strange place but man's abode of refuge and rest. And when you leave this life you do not go to a strange place, but you travel the familiar paths to a place wherein you have lived before. Aye, death leads you home from your long and weary journey.

"Once your earthly bodies slept securely in the bosom of the earth until the warm sun rays penetrated the crust and quickened the dormant sinews and clothed you with a temporal garment.

"Death and life are like the darkness and the twilight. They nest together but never embrace one another. Aye, they are like two strange wayfarers who lodge in the same inn but never speak to one another. They are two rivals but not two enemies. For that which life causes to integrate, death causes it to disintegrate. And the change is the secret of life and death.

"The same gentle fingers that have opened the petal in the spring close it during the cold months of autumn. And just as the cold autumn had dried the rose and the air robbed it of its colors and the wind scattered its precious perfume, the warm April, the month of blossoms, will adorn it again, and will cause more roses to bloom. Verily, I say unto you, life is death in bloom, and death is life in the stillness.

"Death and life are like the two ends of the same measuring rod. Aye, they are the two silent partners who harmoniously work together.

"While you are living you are imprisoned in a house of clay, but when you die, you are released like a bird that escapes the snare of the fowler and is on the wing flying in endless space. When your souls leave, your mortal bodies are left like a deserted booth in an autumn vineyard garden.

"Once freed, the wings of your soul can ride on the ether and your inner eyes can see the outermost end of the universe, and the stars and the planets will be your constant companions. You will enter by the same door through which you left and saw the first light of the sun. Your incarnated souls will dance on the circle chain of eternity and the past yesterday and the distant tomorrow will merge in the silence of endless time, and the measuring rod of days, months, and years will hide beyond the distant stars.

"Verily, I say to you, gods, like the seas, give and take, and they love to drink of the vine of life that their own hands have planted, and breathe the breath which their own nostrils have exhaled. Let birth and death grasp hands and rejoice together, for one is the beginning and the other the end.

"When you are dying, say, 'I have drunk from the sweet and bitter Cup of Life and now my journey is over. I came in peace and in peace I go.' Truly, I say unto you, the same gentle hands that brought you into this world are able to receive you again, and the same nostrils that exhaled you are waiting to inhale you again. And the invisible force

The Tenth Scroll: About Death

that caused the inanimate matter to speak and walk will carry you through space on its wings.

"Awake! Awake, oh thou that sleepest, my messenger is ready to knock at your door. Why doest thou fear death, oh man; why doest thou dread to drink from the cup from which myriads have drunk before you? Drink from the cup and trust in God the Creator—the owner of the Great Vineyard.

"When a child is born, the Lord of Life is there; and when the candle of life is put out, He is still standing there. Aye, He is there in the month of the blossoms to watch and guide the opening of the tender flower. He is there when the leaves of the tree fall off. Silent is the sound of His footsteps and sweet and sad are the tones of His flute.

"And then say, 'Now, I know that my earthly mantle is worn out and my clay vessel is breaking up, and the precious fragrance is dripping. And now my soul is drifting aimlessly, seeking directions to cross the unknown sea.'

"And then offer thanks and say, 'Oh, how many times Thou hast lighted my lamp. And countless times Thou hast put it out, only to light it again.'

"Oh, my beloved ones, how can I explain death to you? Can darkness speak of the light, or can a blind man describe the colors of flowers?"

CHAPTER 13

The Eleventh Scroll: About Freedom

When the morning was riding on the wings of dawn, there was a brief silence, and another scroll opened, and its contents were about freedom. And the man of God opened his mouth and read:

"Your yearning for freedom is the echo of your lost songs, and dreams of a new one. Verily, I say unto you, your precious harp is broken and your fingers have lost their touch on the strings of your heart. But your heart still feels the silent rhythm of past melodies and your feet are ready to dance at the lost sound of the flute.

"Aye, I liken you to an eagle with broken wings resting on a rock and dreaming of the days when he was the master of the air. So even you, every once in a while, flap your wings and try to fly to the land of your dreams. And as you rise from the ground, you breathe the breath of freedom, and for a while you are freed from the chains that bind you to this earth; and you hear new but familiar voices, and behold images of perfection.

"Yea, these images are the shadows of your real self, and the songs are the tones which you once played upon the harp of your heart with harmony and joy. They come back to you when you tune yourselves with the infinite and in spirit become one with the universe.

"In truth, I say unto you, your thoughts of freedom, abundance, peace, and health are the hidden fragrance made from the flowers of the garden that you had left. The fence is broken and the garden is trampled upon and the wild animals have devoured it, but the fragrance is still in the air. Aye, the plants are gone, but the delicate taste of their fruit is still nesting in your palate. And as long as you cherish those past memories and your palate feels the sweet taste, you will dream of your lost freedom and try to see a new horizon.

"Verily, I say unto you, the sun and the moon laugh at you when they see you searching for that which you already

The Eleventh Scroll: About Freedom

hold in your hand and praying to gods for that which you already possess.

"Aye, freedom is something so precious that no one can bestow it upon you. Freedom is not even within the reach of kings. The wise have sought it in books; the prophets in dreams and visions, and the rich merchants have searched for it in far-off lands beyond the seas, but all of them have failed to find it. The secret of freedom is in your own mind and its seat is in your own heart.

"If you wish to be free no one can restrain you; no, not even the gods were able to stop you when you broke a branch from the Tree of Life in which you had nested when you were in the Garden of Eden.

"The trees of the forest patiently stand firm on the ground. Stars and planets spin in their fixed orbits from everlasting to everlasting and animals have no choices. But you are free like the air and like the wind you can change the course of your life.

"In truth, I say unto you, the key to freedom and prison is fashioned with your own hands, and the same hand that locks the door can also open it again. And the seeds of freedom still rest in your heart, and the force that causes you to descend will not help you to ascend, but the power that will cause you to rise and recover your lost freedom is greater than the force that caused you to fall.

"The water does not rise above its source. Your government, whether it be good or bad, is you. Aye, you have chosen the seed and planted it. All those who share in the booty are the partners of the raiders. The net in which you have been entangled was designed, spun, and woven with your own fingers. All of the enslaved people have enslaved themselves. The worm that destroys a tree is nourished by roots and the tender leaves thereof.

"Freedom is a gift of God bestowed upon man and it is an honor given the wise and the brave.

"All the king's children are princes and born free, but not all of them retain their freedom; some relapse into servitude while others bring a harsh yoke upon their own necks and bind their own hands with the fetters they fashion with their own fingers.

"Man can be free but he cannot be equal. All men cannot be princes—neither can all men be servants. Verily, I say unto you, true freedom is like air and sunshine, free and abundant for all.

"Great is man's love for a woman, but his love for freedom is greater and his desire is a flaming fire."

CHAPTER 14

The Twelfth Scroll: About Time

And when the sun had thrown its golden canopy over the summit of the mountain and the dawn changed to light, another scroll opened, and its contents were about time. And the man of God opened his mouth and read:

"Waves move with patience to their destination; winds seek direction, but time is still. It has neither destination nor direction nor beginning nor end. Time was neither created nor is subject to death. Time which we know exists only in mind. As the earth turns on its axis and moves in space, the unseen thread on which events are strung unwinds itself, and past events like precious stones in a necklace shine in space.

"Every minute that the earth travels around the sun new events are unfolded and new things come to light. Verily, I say unto you, time was manifest when God created the sun, the moon, and the stars.

"In time one sees himself only in the past and his own shadow in the distant future. For only the warmth of the sun separates sowing from reaping, and only the spinning of the earth divides yesterday from the distant tomorrow, and life from death.

"In truth, I say unto you, life is a short dream in daytime, and time is like a fleeting shadow at eventide. Yea, shadows are its footsteps; light and darkness are its hidden wings. Time moves silently over boundless space and to its inarticulate voice respond all the creatures.

"Stealthily comes and stealthily goes, and yet, the sound of its hidden wheels causes hearts to tremble, and to its sweet melodies responds all creation. Aye, time begins where it ends and it ends where it begins. And when time silences one voice millions of other voices wait for their turn to greet the alluring sound of its footsteps. Verily, I say unto you, time's left hand is on the plow and with its right hand it holds the sickle.

"Oh, you brothers and sisters, once I dwelled in your

The Twelfth Scroll: About Time

earthly home, my flesh and sinews were of your flesh and sinews. And I drank the cup from which you drink and sang my songs upon your harp, and I walked the narrow and the steep paths that your feet trod.

"Earth was the temple of my soul, and the light of the sun and the stars my lamp, and time was my teacher and pathfinder. When the dark shadows lengthened their canopy upon the earth, it reminded me of my prayers and place of refuge. Its gentle and formless touch awakened me in the morning to give praise to the Guardian of my soul.

"But now I live in the stars, and the sun and the moon are below me, and time has fled to its eternal place and it hides itself in eternity. Aye, now I can see the imprints of my feet on the sky and upon the calm waves of the sea. Now future is my present and time is my vanished dream.

"Verily, I say unto you, time is a companion that no one has given in marriage; it is a servant for whom no master has bargained, and a wayfarer whom no one has invited to lodge under his roof. Yet time lives with you, walks with you, and at night it embraces you in its arms. Time reminds you of the season of seeding and pruning, and of the months of harvest and ingathering. It heralds the warm and soothing winds of the spring, and warns you of the bitter cold of winter.

"Aye, time is your hope in sorrow and your joy in success. Time stays with you until the great curtain is lifted, and past and future are united. Then it gently leads you on your journey to your eternal rest, and flies back to its eternal place.

"Oh, how silent is the sound of its feet and how small is its voice. And yet its warnings are heeded by the birds of the air and the fish of the sea. Oh, how sweet and sorrowful is its music. The sweet sound of its tones cause plants and trees to dance, the flowers to open their precious vessels and to empty their sweet perfume.

"Time places jeweled crowns on the heads of men when it is rightly and wisely used; but it also fills men's cups with bitter tears.

"The habitation of time is in the Milky Way, and stars and planets are the jewels in its crown, and its starlit scepter is the sun and the moon. Aye, time is sought in the skies and yet is found slowly and gently walking in the shadow of the cliffs and the trees of the forest. When you try to behold time in the daylight you will find it standing in the darkness; when you search for it during the night, it is waiting for you in the twilight. Yea, when time marches forward you can see it standing behind you.

"In truth, I say unto you, the king may grace your dwelling place once or twice, but time is your guest only once. Therefore, when you awake embrace it in your arms, for time never looks behind or listens to those who have refused to greet the sound of its feet and listen to the rhythm of its drum."

CHAPTER 15

Crossing the Line into the Unknown

And when the sun had lightened the mountains and the valley and the shepherds were leading their sheep to distant pastures, then the man of God placed the scrolls in a worn leather bag, and said:

"The words which your inner ear has heard and the visions you have seen near this sacred stone and the words which I have read from these ancient scrolls will surely be fulfilled, just as buds on a fruit tree open and grow into mature fruit. In the solitude and silence of night when time and space vanish, your spiritual eyes have seen the unseen and your inner ears have heard the inarticulate tongues of the angels. And now the light has replaced the darkness and the verdant valley is singing praises to the God of Light.

"A new day has been born, and it has brought upon its wings hope and happiness. I have read all the scrolls which I have in my possession—the oracles that I received when I was in quest of wisdom and understanding and when I meditated on the life hereafter and the unknown."

Then he cried out in a loud voice and said:

"Awake, awake! O you who sleep, the light has replaced the darkness. Awake and depart in peace, and let the peace of God go with you. Let the words which you have heard nestle in your hearts, and let them be spoken to generations to come.

"Verily, I say unto you, on this high summit you have transcended your earthly aspirations when at this oracle you took refuge in the silence of the night. You have seen time vanish and the past and the future join hands. Aye, you have reached the distant shores of your heart's desires and the borders of your imagination.

"In truth, during the silent and dark hours of night, your souls have wandered in timeless space and have bathed in the infinite Ocean of Life. And at the dawning you saw the fulfillment of your distant dreams."

Then he cried again, but this time in a low and melancholy voice, with deep emotion, and said:

"Arise! Start on your long journey of life and let your heart nourish your dreams and let time bear them on its wings, and let the gentle winds scatter them beyond the seas.

"You came here to seek wisdom so that you may see a glimpse of the unknown, and I have given you understanding so that you may unlock the mysteries of nature and speak in the tongue of angels. Aye, for a while during the night you transcended this material world of realities and have seen new horizons and have wandered in infinite space.

"Now as you descend to the verdant valley, greet the shepherds who watch over their flocks and say to them, 'Just as you keep tender and careful watch over your sheep, so the Great Shepherd of Life is watching over you.' And to the sower in the field, say, 'May your dreams of today be fulfilled tomorrow, and may the precious seed which you scatter on the ground be multiplied.' And to the reaper say, 'Your hopes of the spring have been fulfilled in the summer and you are ingathering that which your hand has scattered in faith and confidence, and mother earth has nourished the precious seed in its bosom and multiplied it a hundredfold for you, and to bless those who share it with you.'"

And as they were awaking, he blessed them, saying:

"Blessed is the womb that bore you; blessed are the breasts that nourished your hungry sinews. Blessed are the memories of your departed ones which brought you here to this sacred stone."

An elderly scribe whose inner ear had hearkened to the wondrous revelations of the man of God and whose inner eye had seen each scroll open, spoke in his sleep, saying, "Oh learned seer, tell us where is the unknown." And the man of God answered:

"Life is like a circle—it has no beginning and no end. Yet seemingly it has a beginning in the blossom and an end in the fruit. There is a beginning and an end to your body but not to your spirit."

Then he continued:

"Let me tell you, when I came to the end of my journey and entered the last inn to wait for my turn to cross into the unknown, I heard many noble and wise guests who had been waiting, speak. Some of them were praising what they had done and glorying in positions they had held in their life. Others were blaming God for their misfortunes and still others sat speechless because of the fear of the unknown.

"A sage who had been waiting in the last inn had spoken and had said, 'Blessed be the Creator who clothed me with flesh and sinews and quickened me and made me to start on this long and mysterious journey.' Then he added, with a faint smile, 'I am not afraid to cross the dreaded dark line which we see ahead of us into the unknown, for I know my Creator who created the known is also the Lord of the unknown. Yea, I do not remember how I came into this life and I am not afraid of my departure.'

"All the people stared at him and held their hands on their mouths, wishing that he would speak again. And when silence had reigned for a time in the inn, the sage spoke again, 'I have drunk of the sweet and bitter Cup of Life, my cup has been full, and my portion from the king's table. Aye, while I am waiting with you in this dreadful inn I have seen God's shadow upon the mountains, His imprint on the desert, and His paths upon the seas. I have heard His silent voice amid fear and mournful cries. For in this strange and fearful inn crowns and honors are cast to the ground and the prince and the slave lie side by side. Yet in truth, even in this fearful abode, I have felt the touch of His fingers and I have seen the radiant smile of His face, and I have held the hem of His starlit mantle.

"'In the dreams of my childhood, when I was pure and my innocence ascended as a sweet offering before Him, when my oil was plentiful and my lamp was burning, I heard His voice calling me and telling me to be ready to depart because the day was spent and the night was nigh and a new guest had arrived at the inn to occupy my place.

"'And as I grew older I could hear His voice louder and louder, saying, "Awake! Awake, O thou wayfarer, be ready to start on your journey while the day is young and while the sun is in the skies and while your flickering lamp is still burning; before the messenger of the Innkeeper knocks at your door; before the light of your lamp is snuffed away because of the lack of oil."

"'Aye, in all my journey to this last inn my heart was moved by His inarticulate songs, and at times His formless fingers played upon the harp of my soul to strengthen me, and His sweet melodies caused the songs of my youth to merge into the melodies of my manhood, and the joys of boyhood to blossom in my old age. Yea, He was always nigh to me wherever I went, and the sound of His silent footsteps were heard by my inner ear.'

"Then he stretched out his hands as though imploring God, and said, 'In vain is our struggle to keep our flickering lamps burning amid storms and turbulent winds. In vain are our fears and worries.' Then he continued, 'Let us be ready, and depart while our lamps are burning; before the Great Judge sends His messengers to deliver the dreaded summons!

"'You cried at your birth before your eyes could see the light of the sun, yea, before you had a glimpse of this world. Verily, I say unto you, you will cry again. But when you cross the dreaded dark line and see the light, some of you will rejoice but others will mourn.'

"Then he said, 'I am not afraid to cross the line into the unknown because I know Him. With my prayers in meditation I have touched His scepter adorned with myriads of stars and in silent prayers I have entered into His hidden chambers. In solitude and the stillness of night I have listened to His voice whispering like the autumn winds whisper through the rustle of the dry leaves heralding the cold months of the winter.'

"There was a grim silence in the inn; the wayfarers continued to stare at one another with awe but no one dared to speak. Then a wise man looked at the sage and said,

'Your wise words have made us think and to reconsider all that which we have learned in the light of what you have told us. Now can you tell us something about the life behind this door which we are waiting for our turn to cross through?'

"Then the sage spoke again, and said, 'Why are you so fearful to cross the line into the unknown? You were born to die in order to live forever. Can a tree regret that it has brought forth leaves and blossoms? Can the reaper weep over the ripened grain which he cuts with his sickle? Can a butterfly turn back into the cocoon which it has deserted? Can the wheel of life be turned backward?

"'In truth, your fearful thoughts of another life beyond this inn in which you are now waiting to take the cup into your trembling hands and to drink the last drops of life are motivated by the dark shadows of the imperfect temple which your earthly hands have built for the Lord of Life and your wishes to build a better one.

"'Once in my solitude and meditation I heard a strange voice crying to a group of weary builders who were examining the palace they had built for their beloved king. One of the expert masons while looking at the palace had seen a few defects in a wall thereof and mournfully said, to the other masons, "I wish we had done this and not done that." And as the builders were bemoaning their mistakes a master mason spoke and said, "Brother masons, hearken unto me: A tree is well satisfied both with its leaves and its blossoms. Neither in the spring nor in the summer does it condemn that which its roots had dreamed and designed during the cold winter months. Instead of regrets it offers all of its perfume to the God of Life, who has endowed it with wisdom and adorned it with glory and majesty. Only God, the Creator, can make a perfect tree and build a flawless palace.

" ' "Now let me tell you, what we have wrought for our king is good enough for the time being, but let us learn from our mistakes. Then when the king commands us to build him another palace, we will do better."

" 'Then another mason spoke and said, "Oh, brother masons, what if after we have gone away, the king does not summon us again to build him another palace—a better one? What would posterity think of us?"

" ' "Well," answered the master mason, "if the king should need a better palace, he will summon us again." He thoughtfully added, "Oh, brother masons, the mortal is dead while he is alive, and the immortal in death is free from the shackles of time and space. Aye, the formless does not take form; the dweller of the tent is not woven into the fabric of his tent. Verily, I say unto you, your soul and body dwell together, but they are strangers one to another. They are like two strangers who have struck an acquaintance on a long road, but who are always mindful of the crossroads and byways which may cause them to part from one another."

" 'Then a stranger, another master mason, spoke and said, "Brother masons, permit me to say a word and to impart to you some of the wisdom which I have gained. In silence I have listened to you, and with patience I have pondered over your wise words, but now let me ask you: Why do you worry about a temporary earthly abode—a shepherd's tent? Yea, no matter how many times you are hired by the king and how many times you return to build him a better palace, you will never build one in which your eyes would not behold some defects.

"'"In truth, I say unto you, perfection is not within the reach of mortal men but belongs to the God of Life. You will never be pleased with the temporal abodes you build. Aye, your true palaces are the good works you have done and have left behind to posterity. Let the King of Kings examine your work and reward you accordingly. Now let the scroll of life close and let the black curtain be lowered, for soon another curtain is to rise and another world is to unfold itself."'

"Such was the wisdom I heard when I sat in the last inn, and such was the dread and uncertainty which was felt by those who were on their journey to cross the dark line," said the man of God.

"And now, people of my blood and my flesh, as you march through life, new scenes and panoramas will unfold before your mortal eyes. And as you move from one scene to another in your long journey to what you call the unknown, new worlds will unfold and new dimensions of life will appear to you. And when you come to the end of your journey you will find that which is now unknown is known. For life is a circle; it ends where it begins, and begins where it ends. Wherever the sun sets, the dawn breaks."

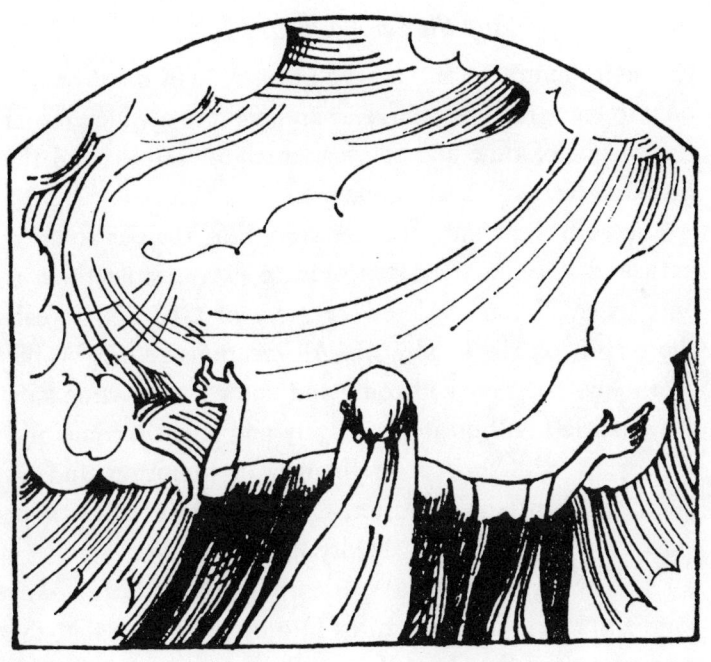

CHAPTER 16

The Hereafter

And it came to pass as the man of God finished speaking on the unknown, he started to explain the hereafter. And he opened his mouth and with a brief sigh, as though he was reluctant to speak on such a subject, he said:

"The thoughts of the hereafter have wearied my soul and caused my sleep to flee. I wandered in this valley and on the high mountains and prayed in solitude in quest of wisdom to know the hereafter. Day and night in my meditation the weight of time and the fear of the unknown and the hereafter have laid heavy upon me.

"In truth, I say unto you, for everything there is an open path and a well-marked exit; and to every riddle there is an answer. Nature declares the glory of God and reveals the secrets of His handiwork. All creations return by the same way that they had come and enter by the same gate they had left. All creatures bravely and silently come and silently go with no fear or thought of tomorrow and no question about the hereafter. Like the green and tender grass they come and like the dry stubble they go.

"The water slowly and patiently finds its way to its source, the sea. The dust turns into more dust so that the magic touch of the Great Potter's fingers may fashion other vessels. All natural things know that their span of life is like a weaver's web that is cut off when it is finished; and like wayfarers, they are mindful of their departure. The plants store the rays of the sun for the time being and turn them into food, and then let them decay and return to the sun again. From whence they came thither, they go."

He paused, as if gathering his thoughts, and then he spoke again and said, "As the shadows were lengthening and the day darkening and the time of my departure from this temporal life was nigh, the thought of death and the fear of the hereafter haunted me, not so much because of the fear of dying, but because I dreaded the unknown and the life hereafter. I was ready to leave the known and blindly cross the turbulent sea in a ship without a rudder and with no haven in view. And I prayed that the fear which had shut the doors of my vision might be removed, but I found that the more I meditated on the hereafter, the more the dread in my heart increased, and my vision became obscured. Then said I to myself, Would that I had been born blind so that I might not have seen the light of the sun and the beauty of this life, and so that the thoughts of the hereafter might not have laid so heavy upon me.

"Yet in truth, it is only a thin curtain, spun by the fingers of nature and woven on the mysterious loom of time, which hides the known from the unknown, separates the now from the hereafter, the blossom from the fruit, and the sower from the reaper. You have no remembrance of the place from which you came, neither of the day when you first saw the light. Aye, you left the dark and the unknown and opened your eyes unto the known, and you were received like the calm water of a long meandering stream when it reaches its destination, the sea. It knows nothing of its source but calmly merges with the water from which it came, and from which it will emerge again. You came naked and devoid of knowledge and naked and full of knowledge shall you return.

"During your sojourn in this world, you have seen that nature has a single pattern, yea, only one and not two or three. You have learned that the gods of nature have perfect scales and balances, and a single and straight measuring rod for all creations. Now, on this uncertain journey, you will see how the wise and the prudent become speechless, and how the prophet and the seer are helpless in the face of the thoughts of eternity.

"Now, my brethren and my kinsmen, incline your ear and hearken unto me. In truth, all other creations take this final journey of life bravely, without thought or fear of the life hereafter, and they drink from life's cup like valiant men when they march into the battle with faith and confidence in victory.

"Does the tender and colorful rose know where the wind and storm will hurl its dry petals, or where the breeze will carry its precious scent? Yea, they come quietly and they go quietly, praising the God of Life who adorns them with beauty and glory and then strips them naked and sends them away empty. Aye, they still live secure in the seed of their kind, which they tenderly had nourished, and that will continue to grow and grace the earth to the end of time. And they are mindful that the same gentle and formless hands that planted them have cut them off and will plant them again."

And it came to pass, after a few minutes of silence he spoke again and said, "In vain is your anxiety about the life hereafter. There is an end to man's mortal mind, a limit to his imagination. Oh man, the door of the hereafter is hidden from your eyes, and your journey is on a tractless road with no footprints on the ground nor guideposts to point the way. The reclining shadows of death and the hereafter, your eyes shall never behold; nor can your mortal mind compass the width of the universe and the heights of the heaven.

The Hereafter

Can a drop of dew in a desert reveal the vastness of the ocean? Can a man empty a sea with a spoon?"

Then he spoke again and said, "On my arrival at the crossing line which separates the life here from the life hereafter, I was impatient to cross before the messenger of death delivered his dreaded summons. Bravely I drew near the border line trying to get a glimpse of the hereafter, and lo, suddenly a strange man with a fierce countenance appeared before me, and cried with a loud voice and said, 'Do not attempt to cross the line, your turn has not yet come, the weight of time is still upon you.' And I looked, and lo, the strange figure was standing between the light and the darkness, between the known and the hereafter. His apparel was half white and half dark; one of his feet was over the white line and the other over the dark line.

"After I had fearfully observed the strange phenomenon, I said to him, trembling, 'Who are you, my lord?' and he answered, 'I do not know who I am. All I know is that some pilgrims call me life, and others call me death. You can see, I stand with one foot in the light and the other foot in darkness.'

"Then I besought him to tell me what was beyond the dark line, and where was the hereafter. In bewilderment he answered, 'I do not know what kind of life is beyond the dark line for I have never crossed these lines. I have been standing where you see me stand before the earth started to revolve around the sun; yea, before the first shafts of light fell upon it, I was standing here to light the candles that are held in the hands of the myriads of wayfarers who cross the dark line into the light, and to put out the candles of those who cross the white line into the dark.'

"Then I said to him, 'Oh guardian of life and death, I beseech you, tell me where all of these people come from and whither they go.' And he replied, 'This is a secret hidden in a sealed scroll which no one can open, yea, not even the prophets and seers, but only the Lord of Life, Himself, who is also the Lord of Death and the Hereafter.'

"And when I awoke I found that it was a revelation. Soon my long-awaited summons came and I was happy to depart.

"Now in truth, I say unto you, in my quest for the life hereafter, I have found that this mortal life is a replica of the life hereafter. Death is nothing but an eternal change, an infinity, and the life hereafter begins right now. The little acorn which once was held and nourished by the tender bough, is buried in the ground and becomes a large oak tree to bear more acorns on its boughs.

"Verily, I say unto you, even after you have crossed the white line into the dark and the dreaded unknown, you will see the light of His countenance penetrating the grave, and hear the small voice even in the solitude of the earth. Aye, it was in the grim silence and thick darkness that your body was conceived and fashioned and in which the immortal and the mortal joined hands to dance in a timeless space. Out of a sunless and starless universe you emerged and in the stillness of time you shall depart carrying your burning candle in your hand. For out of the darkness comes forth light, and out of the light, immortality.

"In truth, life is like a candle from which myriads of

candles are lighted. And, even though all light appears the same, there is a difference, for not two candles are alike. All the grains of sand are similar, but no two are alike. Consider the flowers of the field: some of them are graced with beauty and majesty, worthy to be placed on the king's table. But some, even though they are clothed with glorious colors, are thorny. Yet, they are still cultivated by the same Gardener and nourished by the same hidden forces and watered by the same stream.

"In death and in life man's identity is eternal. Consider the precious diamonds: they all have brilliant colors, but are diverse, one from another. Aye, there are not two leaves on a tree which are alike, neither do two flakes of snow contain the same design. Verily, I say unto you, every man is an eternal flower with a different scent in the Great Garden of the God of Life.

"Life cannot be weighed on scales, nor separated into forms or degrees, for life is measureless, embracing all, and is manifested in diverse forms and degrees. Life was never created, nor will it die. In truth, life is the eternal wine made from the vine planted by the fingers of God to be drunk by angels and men, by mortals and immortals, by the saints and the sinners. And, being so great and precious, it is hidden even from the eyes of the angels.

"Verily, I say unto you, the secret of the hereafter is buried in its own seed. Yea, the riddle is beyond the comprehension of the wise and the prudent. The life hereafter is the dream of today fulfilled tomorrow, and man, being a spark of life, cannot explain the secret of life. How can a vessel understand the potter, its maker, or describe the touch of his gentle fingers? How can the leaves explain the intricate design the roots have woven in the dark and hidden chambers of the ground? Only life can disclose its secret. Only the sea can feel the weight of the water which it contains, and only the wings can measure the thinness of the air.

"Aye, the hereafter is hidden in the bygone yesterday, and the secret of today in the unborn tomorrow, and the riddle of eternity is hidden in the beginning. Life lives with those who know how to live and dies with those who know how to die, and is born with those who are born, and sleeps with those who sleep in the dust, to raise them again to life.

"The Cup of Life is full and running over; its suns never set, its dawns never darken, and its horizons are limitless."

The Published Books of Dr. George M. Lamsa

(Some of these books are not currently in print. Please write for information to DeVorss & Company, P.O. Box 550, Marina del Rey, California 90291.)

SECRET OF MIDDLE EAST (1923)
THE OLDEST CHRISTIAN PEOPLE (1926)
KEY TO ORIGINAL GOSPEL (1931)
THE BOOK OF PSALMS (1939)
THE FOUR GOSPELS FROM ARAMAIC TEXT (1933)
THE SHEPHERD OF ALL (1932)
NEW TESTAMENT ORIGIN (1947)
GEMS OF WISDOM (1939)
MY NEIGHBOR JESUS (1932)
THE SHORT KORAN (1949)
THE GOSPEL LIGHT (1939)
THE NEW TESTAMENT . . . FROM ARAMAIC MANUSCRIPTS (1933)
NEW TESTAMENT COMMENTARY (1945)
THE HOLY BIBLE . . . FROM ANCIENT ARAMAIC MANUSCRIPTS (1957)
MORE LIGHT ON THE GOSPEL (1968)
THE HIDDEN YEARS OF JESUS (1968)
MAN FROM GALILEE (1970)
THE SCROLL OPENED (1967)
THE KINGDOM ON EARTH (1966)
OLD TESTAMENT LIGHT (1964)
ROSES OF GULISTAN (1971)
IDIOMS IN THE BIBLE EXPLAINED (1973)